Thoughtful Gestures

Thoughtful Gestures

Words and
Gifts That
Say You Care

Daria Price Bowman

FRIEDMAN/FAIRFAX
P U B L I S H E R S

A FRIEDMAN/FAIRFAX BOOK

©1998 by Michael Friedman Publishing Group, Inc.

Library of Congress Cataloging-in-Publication data available upon request.

ISBN 1-56799-682-5

Editor: Francine Hornberger
Art Director: Jeff Batzli
Designer: Kirsten Berger
Photography Director: Christopher C. Bain
Photography: ©Bill Milne
Prop Stylist: Candace Clark
Production Manager: Jeanne E. Hutter
Illustrations on pages 15 and 45: ©Kirsten Berger

Color separations by Bright Arts Graphics (S) Pte Ltd.
Printed in Singapore by KHL Printing Co Pte Ltd

10 9 8 7 6 5 4 3 2 1

For bulk purchases and special sales, please contact:

Friedman/Fairfax Publishers
Attention: Sales Department
15 West 26th Street
New York, New York 10010
212/685-6610   FAX 212/685-1307

Visit our website:
http://www.metrobooks.com

To

Beverlee Ciccone
and Patricia McKearn

❧ ❧

Michael Friedman Publishing Group
gratefully acknowledges
Dimensions Inc., Reading, Pennsylvania,
for prop used in the photograph on page 40.

Contents

Introduction

Little deeds of kindness,
Little words of love,
Help to make earth happy
Like the heavens above.

—Julia Fletcher Carney

Thoughtful gestures are the small gifts, words, notes, favors, and acts that add pleasure and happiness to our lives. They help us to share joyous occasions, commemorate important happenings, and give a little of ourselves to friends and loved ones. They are little demonstrations of love and caring, acts of kindness, compassion, and courtesy. Thoughtful gestures are the special actions of a thoughtful person, extensions of good manners and courteous behavior.

But a thoughtful gesture goes beyond etiquette and courtesy. It represents a sincere and unselfish deed, done for the sole reason of making the recipient feel special, important, esteemed, or loved. Sometimes the gesture is as small as a friendly smile and a wave to a neighbor or a child in a passing car, or an offer to pick up a few things at the grocery store. It may be the act of generously passing on a bulging file of college application information collected for one's own children to those who are about to take the plunge.

At other times the thoughtfulness is expressed in a grander gesture—perhaps establishing a scholarship to honor a deceased relative or organizing a parade to commemorate a friend's accomplishment. Or it could be sitting for hours in a doctor's office with an elderly neighbor so that she will have the reassurance of a familiar face after frightening medical tests.

> *Only a life lived for others is a life worthwhile.*
>
> *Albert Einstein*

7

Most of us are fortunate to have one special friend or relative who was born with a thoughtful, giving nature, a person who always remembers our birthdays and anniversaries and somehow manages to find the time to send a card or select a befitting gift. These are the ones who clip out newspaper articles and send chocolate chip cookies to a friend's children who are away at school, who make the time to visit sick friends in the hospital on the way home from the office, who pick up the dry cleaning for a colleague who must work late but needs a special suit for a weekend event, and who never fail to send a note of condolence or congratulations. These are the people who organize a committee to create a park in memory of

An effort made for the happiness of others lifts us above ourselves.

Lydia M. Child

a legendary community member and who write letters to the editor praising the local softball team's efforts in the playoffs.

I am especially fortunate to have several such people in my life and I have dedicated this book to two of them, Patricia McKearn and Beverlee Ciccone.

Pat is a dear friend and my business partner. She filled my refrigerator with casseroles when I was recuperating from an illness, took my girls shopping for a Father's Day gift when I was traveling, walked my dog when I was out of town, helped me plant trees and shrubs in my garden when I was racing with a garden tour deadline, sent a funny card covered with signatures to my daughter after her knee surgery, and

8

presented me with a purple butterfly bush for no other reason than because she knew I would love it. Instinctively knowing when something's wrong, Pat is quick to console or commiserate.

Beverlee shares her considerable wisdom and warm and generous nature with my entire family. I can count on her to rescue me from computer fatigue with an impromptu invitation to lunch, to listen to my venting when things don't go my way, and to gently suggest ways to get around a

problem. And despite a schedule that would leave me reeling, Bev always finds the time to observe birthdays and other occasions, large and small, and to find a funny card or T-shirt that perfectly suits any specific situation.

In the past, before shopping malls, computerized mail-order businesses, and entrenched consumerism, people were more apt to demonstrate their affection and esteem by making heartfelt gestures rather than with objects, and gifts were more likely to be of the unique homemade or homegrown variety rather than something mass-produced. Men and women would exchange love letters and poems. Children would gather wildflowers to fashion into daisy chains for their mothers. They also would perhaps bring a shiny red apple to school to present as a token of affection to a favorite teacher.

> *You know very well that love is, above all, the gift of oneself.*
>
> *Jean Anouilh*

Sailors away on extended trips would fashion tokens of their love from seashells to send to their sweethearts at home. Women would spend hours stitching friendship and wedding quilts and would braid locks of a deceased relative's hair for lockets and charms to give to grieving family members.

Most of us have more than enough love and caring in our hearts to share with others. But just like having good manners and behaving courteously, the ability to make thoughtful gestures doesn't necessarily come naturally. It's not that we don't care enough; it's that sometimes we don't know exactly how to show how much we really do care.

Love is the most precious thing in all the world. Whatever figures in second place doesn't come even close.

Ann Landers

The following pages present a variety of examples of ways to demonstrate love and concern for others through special gifts and actions. There are gifts that grow, which show how trees and flowers can become symbols for our caring. There are lots of ideas for handmade tokens of love and ways to prepare food to express what is in your heart. There are exciting ways to commemorate special occasions. You'll find inspiration and ideas to bring joy, laughter, and love to other people's lives with unusual, clever, and caring gestures.

The rest is up to you: act on these ideas and your efforts will be well rewarded.

11

Special Gifts for Special Occasions

For happiness brings happiness,
And loving ways bring love,
And giving is the treasure
That contentment is made of.

—Amanda Bradley

early every occasion provides us with the opportunity to present meaningful gifts to people we care about. Though shopping for the perfect gift for someone special can be a frustrating task, it can become a joyous event if we allow ourselves to go beyond purchasing ordinary, expected gifts and offer instead highly individualized and personal remembrances. These will mean far more to the recipient than perhaps a more costly but less thoughtful gift.

In this chapter you'll find suggestions for out-of-the-ordinary gifts and gestures for births, weddings, anniversaries, housewarmings, and other special occasions.

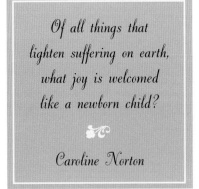

Of all things that lighten suffering on earth, what joy is welcomed like a newborn child?

Caroline Norton

Births, Adoptions, Baby Showers, and Christenings

When my first child, Samantha, was born, a thoughtful gesture from a dear friend sparked a special tradition. She lent me a beautiful handcrafted Pennsylvania Dutch cradle that had been given to her when her first child was born. I loved having the pretty cradle and was delighted to use it again two and a half years later when my daughter Cassandra was born. Since then, a dozen other babies, including my friend's grandchildren, have been rocked to sleep in the cozy cradle. My friend plans to have a special

13

plaque made for it that includes the initials and birthdates of each child who has used the cradle.

When a friend was planning a christening, her godmother offered her own christening gown for the baby to wear. This elaborate gown, which included beautifully detailed under- and overgarments, had been lovingly hand-stitched by her godmother's great-aunts. Having an heirloom gown for my baby to wear made a lovely occasion even more special.

It's not necessary to own, lend, or give heirlooms in order to celebrate the joy new babies bring to our lives. Inspire new traditions by making your own creative and thoughtful gestures. Here are some suggestions:

> *To Janey and Paul,*
> *This certificate is good for ten free nights of babysitting.*
> *Love,*
> *Bea*

- *Collect newspapers with the baby's birthdate and magazines from the same week and month and put them in an attractive* storage box to give to the parents as a simple time capsule. You might include lists of the day's television lineup and the top tunes on the radio.

- *Offer to babysit when the new parents feel ready to spend some time alone. Give a "babysitting gift certificate" that you make yourself.*

- *Give the new baby your favorite childhood book or the one your own children liked best. Be sure to inscribe it with a sentence about why you chose that title and what the book means to you.*

15

WRAP A BOX WITH DECORATIVE PAPER AND RIBBON TRIM TO GIVE TO A NEW MOTHER TO STORE BABY MEMORABILIA.

> *Friendship is the greatest enrichment that I have found.*
>
> 🌿
>
> *Adlai E. Stevenson*

🌺 *Frame a birth announcement in a silver frame and have it engraved with the birthdate to give to the parents.*

🌺 *Send the new parents a gift basket packed with items you've selected personally—they may be purely practical (wipes, a bib, baby socks) or grown-up luxuries (a selection of sweet-smelling bath products for a harried new mom). Whatever you choose will be special because* you *selected it.*

🌺 *If you can't send a gift, send a note with a story to reassure a first-time mom, sharing your own experience or giving a useful tip that only a mom would know.*

🌺 *If you have items from family members' childhoods, offer them as gifts to new or expecting parents.*

🌺 *Present the mother-to-be with the tiny outfit she or the father-to-be wore home from the hospital. If you don't have that outfit, you could present a childhood book or toy.*

🌺 *Find baby photos of the mother- and father-to-be and place them in special frames to give to the new parents on the day the new baby is brought home.*

Engagements, Bridal Showers, and Weddings

Years ago, a young woman I worked with moved back home with her widowed father after she graduated from college. She had agreed to pay rent while she lived there, a situation they were both comfortable with. On her wedding day, her father presented her and her new husband with a check that represented all the rent she had paid during the four years she had lived at home as an adult.

Thoughtful gestures for people in love come in many forms:

🌸 Offer the bride a family heirloom like a string of pearls, a lace handkerchief, or a small prayer book to use as "something old."

🌸 Use your copy of the wedding invitation to decorate the lid of a box or the cover of a photo album. Or you might simply place the invitation in an especially pretty frame.

🌸 Present the couple with an album of candid photos you've taken of them (prewedding parties and the reception offer great opportunities if you don't already have photos).

🌸 Collect the signatures of everyone in the wedding party and use them to decorate a picture frame or the cover of a photo album, or reproduce the signatures on a tray or the lid of a silver box.

PUT TOGETHER AN "EMERGENCY PACK" FOR A BRIDE. FILL IT WITH NECESSITIES
LIKE SAFETY PINS AND CLEAR NAIL POLISH.

Anniversaries

The highlight of one couple's fiftieth wedding anniversary party was a video made from old home movies taken at their wedding. Here are some other lovely ideas for commemorating a special anniversary:

❧ *Offer to babysit the young children of a couple celebrating an anniversary. Have the children spend the night at your house so that the couple will have the simple luxury of a romantic, unhurried evening at home.*

❧ *Send a long-married couple a heartfelt note letting them know how much you admire their commitment.*

❧ *Collect the ephemeral elements of a wedding such as invitations, place cards, favors, monogrammed matches and napkins, and newspaper announcements in a pretty, decorative box and present them to a couple celebrating a first anniversary.*

❧ *Send flowers to a widower or widow on his or her wedding anniversary. Though death has separated the couple, the anniversary still exists and is worthy of being celebrated.*

❧ *Offer to take a widow out for the afternoon or evening.*

Graduations

The president of a graduating class chose to thank the class advisors for their help and support by presenting them each with a class photo. What made the gift especially lovely was that every student had signed the matting surrounding the photo, and some had included brief notes of thanks and appreciation. It's also thoughtful to remember teachers on graduation day.

❧ *Take photos of your graduate with favorite teachers and have duplicate prints made. Send the duplicates to the teachers with a note of thanks.*

PRESENT A COUPLE WITH SILVER CANDLESTICKS TO COMMEMORATE A TWENTY-FIFTH WEDDING ANNIVERSARY.

❧ *Upon graduation, give your child a small photo album with snapshot highlights of his or her student years. If you don't want to part with the original photos, have color copies made to fill the album.*

❧ *Make a scrapbook of report cards, award certificates, newspaper clippings, and other memorabilia from a child's student years to present at graduation.*

❧ *Take out a display ad in your local paper to announce that a friend or family member has earned an advanced degree.*

❧ *Along with a congratulatory card, present a special graduate with a gift certificate for having a degree framed.*

❧ *Encourage a graduating class to make a gift to the school to celebrate their time there. One recent group sponsored an outdoor volleyball court for their school. Others have planted trees. (See chapter 4 for ideas about gifts that grow.)*

Housewarmings

Moving into a new home is often a joyful, though sometimes chaotic, time. It also presents the perfect opportunity to give an old friend or new neighbor a wonderful, thoughtful gift:

❧ *Browse at flea markets and garage sales for vintage linens.*

❧ *Have cocktail napkins printed with the person's new address to give as a small gift.*

❧ *If the house is an old one, search in the county archives for the original deed, make a photocopy of it, and put it in a simple frame to give the new homeowner.*

❧ *Bake a pie and present it to a new neighbor as a gift of welcoming.*

❧ *Have an aerial photo taken of a friend's new house. (Small local airports will help you find someone to take the picture.)*

❧ *Organize a housewarming "shower" for an old friend.*

• *Give a Jewish friend a traditional mezuzah to hang at the front door.*

• *Present a horseshoe to a friend with a new house. The horseshoe is said to bring good luck if it is hung with the curve at the bottom (to keep the luck from falling out).*

• *For a family new to the neighborhood, offer a collection of take-out menus in a colored folder.*

Birthdays and Half-Birthdays

Since birthdays are times when you can usually count on a friend receiving special attention, try to think of something creative—something apart from sending flowers or a card. Also, be sure to keep in mind those people whose birthdays might go unnoticed, such as an older person or a friend whose family lives far away.

One couple I know celebrates half-birthdays for their son, whose birthday is just a few days after Christmas. His half-birthday, however, falls in the summer. It is then that they do the celebration with cake, ice cream, and presents. If you have a child whose birthday falls on or near a major holiday, which will probably divert the attention from his or her special day, institute a tradition in your family of celebrating half-birthdays instead.

One lovely tradition is to save a candle from your child's first birthday cake and use it to adorn future cakes.

21

It is not the weight of jewel or plate,
Or the fondle of silk or fur;
'Tis the spirit in which the gift is rich...

Edmund Vance Cooke

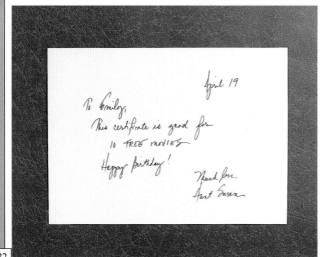

April 19

To Emily,
This certificate is good for
10 FREE MOVIES
Happy Birthday!

Much love,
Aunt Susan

22

Here are some more suggestions for making birthdays special:

🐾 *Ask for tips from the parents of children to whom you want to give a gift. It's so much more meaningful to give the child something he or she will truly enjoy than something you hope he or she might like.*

🐾 *Consider giving gift certificates or even money to teenagers. Though these gifts*

seem impersonal, in most cases they are more likely to be appreciated than something you pick out on your own.

Memorials

Funerals are difficult times for all people concerned. It is sometimes hard to know just what to say or how to act around someone who has just lost a loved one. But your presence at a funeral or sending a heartfelt sympathy card sharing a special memory you have of the person may be all that is needed. Here are some ways others have made the loss more bearable and some suggestions you may want to follow:

🐾 *In a touching and highly personal gesture, a widow distributed hundreds of ties that had belonged to her husband to the large group that attended his memorial service.*

🎀 *For a small memorial for a particularly beloved person, have copies made of a favorite photo of the deceased and distribute them to those who attend the service.*

🎀 *When planning a memorial service, think about following the Quaker tradition of inviting those who have attended to speak a few words.*

Other Special Occasions

🎀 *Collect a program, ticket stubs, promotional flyers, and reviews for a friend or relative who is appearing in a theatrical production.*

🎀 *Create a pretty box or scrapbook in which to store a collection of theatre memorabilia.*

🎀 *Send flowers, a bottle of champagne, or a box of chocolates to the performer's dressing room.*

🎀 *If you take videos of school plays and concerts, soccer games, or other events in which*

other people's children participate, offer to make copies for those who don't have videocameras.

Whenever something happens that is out of the ordinary, be it good or bad, send a note or call to acknowledge it—even the tiniest thoughtful gesture has impact: your thoughtfulness will be remembered long after the event itself has faded from memory.

23

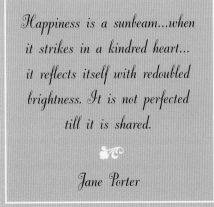

Happiness is a sunbeam...when it strikes in a kindred heart... it reflects itself with redoubled brightness. It is not perfected till it is shared.

Jane Porter

A Word About Wrapping

The smallest gifts become extravagant and wonderful when the wrapping is given special consideration. And it only takes a few more minutes to create a beautifully wrapped package—if you have the right materials. Here's a list of materials you'll always want to have handy:

24

- *A collection of high-quality wrapping papers with plenty of solid colors. These always seem to look elegant. I buy them when they are on sale and store them in a closet.*

- *Ribbon. Buy colors like white, ecru, pale blue, and pale pink in satin, grosgrain, and velvet on large spools in several widths from floral suppliers or at crafts stores. Also collect fancy cording, wired French ribbon, raffia, and festive yarns. Be generous in the amount of ribbon you use. A bow with extra-long "tails" looks extravagant and celebratory.*

- *Decorative additions. Here's where your creativity comes into play. Use a storage box to hold a collection of silk flowers, tassels, lace remnants, bags of confetti, sequins, buttons, tiny toys, shells, faux jewels, dried flowers, cones, pods, fabric trims, stickers, decorative stamps, or any other items that might look pretty or fun atop a gift.*

❧ A huge supply of tissue paper. You can use this for wrapping every type of package, from a shirt box to a gift basket or bag.

❧ Gift bags. These are excellent for wrapping oddly shaped gifts. Make your own from white or colored paper bags adorned with items from your collection of decorative additions.

Here are some other clever, even whimsical ways to present a gift:

❧ Use a vintage ceramic mixing bowl, an old flour canister, or an oversized measuring cup for kitchen or food-related gifts. A woven dish towel can also be used as wrap.

❧ Wrap something small and breakable in several layers of tissue paper, then place it in the foot of a thick, colorful woolen sock. Tie the sock at the ankle with a ribbon or heavy cord.

❧ Adorn packages with a spray of flowers or evergreen twigs from your yard. Flowers will last longest if you put the stems in tiny water-filled vials topped with rubber stoppers. These are available from florists and at floral supply stores.

❧ Decorate plain paper using rubber stamps, colored markers, old snapshots, or what-have-you for a creative, truly personal giftwrap.

CHAPTER
2

Holiday Gifts
and Gestures

Do good and
ask not for whom.

—Yiddish proverb

There is a net of love by which you can catch souls.

Mother Teresa

or many people, holidays represent a joyful time for gathering with friends and relatives. These are the times when we host parties, decorate our homes, and share our good cheer with others. But for some, holidays—and not just the big ones—are a lonely time when other people's merriment only exaggerates their sadness.

In this chapter you will find suggestions for ways to help others experience the joy and fun of holidays. There are also a few ideas for creating special times on obscure holidays.

Christmas and Hanukkah

🪀 *Organize a group of holiday carolers to visit nursing homes, a hospital, or the homes of elderly neighbors. Serve hot chocolate and cookies afterward.*

🪀 *Help the children of divorced or separated parents select or make holiday gifts and cards for their parents. Since this is usually a task taken on by one parent for the other, divorced parents often receive no gifts from their young children, and the children are left feeling that they have somehow let their parents down.*

🪀 *Include a recently widowed or divorced person in your holiday plans. Invite him or her to dinners, parties, and religious observances like lighting the menorah or the candles of an Advent wreath.*

🪀 *Invite a friend or neighbor whose family is far away to attend religious services or enjoy a holiday meal with your family.*

27

Take the time to write personal notes to the people to whom you send holiday greeting cards. It is so much more meaningful to receive a handwritten message than a card with a preprinted or quickly scrawled signature.

In lieu of sending holiday cards to friends, family members, or business associates, make a donation to a special charity in the amount you would usually spend on cards and postage.

Agree with extended family members to forgo sending gifts to now-grown offspring and use the money you would have spent to make a significant donation in the family's name to a charity.

If your work requires around-the-clock job coverage, offer to stand in for a colleague who celebrates different holidays than you.

Organize a drive in your office to donate coats and mittens to a shelter or to be "secret Santas" to underprivileged children by raising a collection for toys.

Veteran's Day and Memorial Day

Hang an American flag at your home. It will mean a great deal to veterans.

Offer to accompany the widow of a veteran to the cemetery to place flowers on the grave.

Visit a veteran's hospital or nursing home and bring along some homemade treats like cookies or apple pies to share.

Thanksgiving

Organize a food drive to benefit a soup kitchen, or volunteer to cook or serve at a shelter.

Invite a student from a foreign country to celebrate this American holiday with your family.

DECORATE AN ORNAMENT TO COMMEMORATE YOUR CHILD'S FIRST CHRISTMAS, AND MAKE DECORATING ORNAMENTS A FAMILY TRADITION FOR YEARS TO COME.

29

🌺 Invite neighbors or coworkers who are unable to join their families to attend your family's Thanksgiving dinner.

Passover

🌺 Host a seder and include friends who are not Jewish so that they may learn more about the history behind the tradition.

🌺 Pack a basket with matzoh, macaroons, wine or grape juice, and other goodies for a friend who might not be able to afford these sometimes expensive Passover treats.

🌺 Offer to help organize a seder at a nursing home or senior center.

> Give what you have.
> It may be better than you think.
>
> Henry Wadsworth Longfellow

Easter

🌺 Plan an Easter egg hunt at a shelter or an institution for ill or troubled children.

🌺 Offer to buy a new Easter outfit for a child through a charitable organization.

🌺 Pack Easter baskets for children whose families can't afford to. Churches or other charitable groups will make sure they are delivered. Instead of lots of candy, add simple gifts and small toys to the baskets. Colored pencils, crayons, tiny notebooks, wind-up toys, little decorative boxes, and stickers are appropriate.

Mother's Day and Father's Day

Many families do not celebrate Mother's Day and Father's Day because they believe that "every day should be Mother's or Father's Day." By that they mean that we should be able to demonstrate our love for our parents without the prompting of a special holiday and all of the commercialism that surrounds it. Nevertheless, for many people these days serve as reminders to send a card, flowers, or a little gift to emphasize that we do care.

Often, the gifts and gestures that are appreciated most and really touch the heart are the simplest ones. Handmade treasures and the memories of lovingly served lukewarm coffee and slightly burned toast are among the things many Moms and Dads cherish most.

> *Instead of hosting a Mother's Day brunch in a crowded restaurant, make Mom all her favorite dishes and serve them to her at her home or yours.*

> *Honor your parents with donations to their favorite charities.*

> *Help young children make breakfast or dinner for their mother or father.*

A gift though small is welcome.

Greek proverb

> *Assist the small children of single parents in creating handmade gifts for their parent or in cooking something special. Ask them what their mother and father like best and help them try to replicate it.*

> *Take flowers to a nursing home or hospital for mothers and fathers who have no visitors.*

> *Send long-distance gift certificates or prepaid phone cards to far-away parents on fixed budgets to let them know that you'd love to hear from them.*

> *Make a special effort for mothers or fathers who have outlived their children. They could be particularly lonely on Mother's or Father's Day.*

31

The calendar is crowded with obscure holidays—some that are observed only by small groups, others that have become more or less forgotten. Books listing holidays and feast days can be found in the library or any bookstore and are useful for those who like to find small reasons to host a party or make a celebration. If you're hooked up to the internet, why not surf around and see what you can come up with?

Look for a holiday and create your own fun with special gifts and gestures to go with it. For example, on Earth Day or Arbor Day, volunteer to help young children plant a tree, or take them on a nature walk. Or, use the pretext of a saint's feast day, a foreign holiday, a poet's birthday, or the anniversary of a news-making event to throw a party, plan a picnic, send a note, or otherwise make a seemingly ordinary day special.

Though we most often wait for a special day to create a celebration—which is really nothing more than taking the time to share ourselves with others—we really don't need to wait for the most appropriate or significant time to do it. By attaching a little importance to relatively insignificant days, we simply increase the opportunities for togetherness and making others happy.

> *Who soweth good seed shall surely reap.*
>
> ❧
>
> *Julia C.R. Dorr*

HELP A CHILD PREPARE AND DECORATE HEART-SHAPED HOMEMADE COOKIES AS A PRESENT FOR MOTHER'S DAY.

Handmade
Is Heartfelt

❦ ❦

*When people take the time and care to
make the presents they give, they put into
the gifts not only the materials needed, but
also a part of themselves. The thoughts and
feelings behind the giving, not the grandness
of the gift, are the important ingredients.*

—Tasha Tudor

hen I was younger, I was part of a group of women that gathered every Wednesday evening, ostensibly to quilt, needlepoint, or embroider. And though we would do some quilting or other handiwork, the true reason we got together was to talk, to share our thoughts and problems, and to spend time together as women have done for centuries, a practice that is hard to keep alive in the fast-paced world we live in today.

A lovely tradition of our little group was to commemorate the birth of our children with a small crib quilt or a cross-stitch sampler, with each member of the group making one of the squares or stitching a section. During the years we created many quilts and samplers, and I treasure the two made for my daughters. Though they are now tucked away with other sentimental treasures, these lovingly crafted pieces remain very dear to my heart.

Over the years, you may have received handmade gifts from your family, including such items as woven baskets, cross-stitch wall hangings,

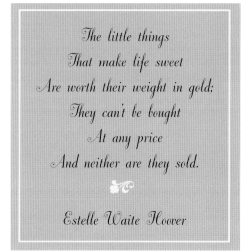

The little things
That make life sweet
Are worth their weight in gold;
They can't be bought
At any price
And neither are they sold.

Estelle Waite Hoover

35

and picture frames, to the more complex, like crib quilts and samplers. You'll find that whatever your skill level, gifts you make yourself will be cherished by those who receive them.

People who are clever with their hands are most likely accustomed to giving the results of their labors to friends and relatives. If you love to knit, crochet, cross-stitch, sew,

patchwork pillows, embroidered hand towels, and Christmas ornaments. And, no doubt, every piece, from the simplest to the most expert, is special, reminding you if dear old friends.

In this chapter, we'll look at small gifts you can make yourself. Handmade treasures range from the very simple, like note cards

do needlepoint, or quilt, or if you are adept with a glue gun, clever with ceramics, or skilled with a saw, you probably already know how much people enjoy receiving your handmade and heartfelt creations as gifts.

It's especially thoughtful to make gifts that are personalized—hand-knit mittens,

'WHAT GRANDMOTHER WOULDN'T CHERISH A BOOK MADE ESPECIALLY BY AN ADORING GRANDCHILD?'

hats, and scarves in a grandchild's favorite colors and adorned with his or her name or initials; a cross-stitched pillow or hanging with a birthdate, an appropriate quote, or the punch line to an inside joke; or a birdhouse painted to match your friend's house.

A young person going away to school might enjoy a coverlet fashioned from his or her old flannel shirts or worn-out jeans. And new mothers will cherish a baby blanket crocheted by hand or a little wooden stool emblazoned with the baby's name.

Anyone can make a handmade gift—even those who claim to be all thumbs. Even if your last handmade gift was the result of a seventh-grade shop project, you can still create a special present for someone you care about. Here are a few projects that range from simple for the beginner to a little more challenging for the experienced crafter:

🐾 *Using a glue gun, attach moss, dried flowers, cones, and pods to the rim of a pretty straw basket. Line the basket with a vintage handkerchief or fancy tea towel and fill it with potpourri, soaps, or candy.*

🐾 *Make a sachet. Cut two squares or rectangles of decorative fabric, place the right sides together, and sew around three sides with a tight running stitch. Cut the top edges with pinking shears and fold inside out, forming a pouch. Fill the pouch with potpourri. Close the pouch with a rubber band and tie a ribbon or cord around the band.*

🐾 *Use a glue gun to decorate inexpensive wooden frames and boxes (available at crafts stores) with sequins, decorative stamps, decoupage cutouts, lace or fabric remnants, ribbons, buttons, shells, or what have you.*

🐾 *For a book lover, make personalized bookmarks with pressed flowers, stamps, magazine cutouts, cut-up photographs, decorative*

37

ribbons, and fabric or lace remnants. Attach the decorations to a piece of cardboard cut to the right size and place between two pieces of laminating plastic (available at hobby stores). Follow directions for laminating (usually as simple as ironing the two pieces together) and trim.

Create a "busy book" for young children to play with when they visit you. Cut several rectangles of brightly colored cotton fabric. Half of each rectangle will be a "page" in the book. Place two rectangles wrong sides together and stitch all the way around with about an inch (2.5cm) of margin. Clip around the margins with pinking shears about one-quarter inch (6mm) from the stitching. Place several of the rectangles— three or four will do—together in a pile. Fold them in half so that the short sides meet and stitch a "spine" about one-quar-

ter inch (6mm) from the fold. Make the book's title with felt or fabric letters and attach with a glue gun, or write on the cover page with fabric markers. Each page should feature an activity like buttoning buttons, snapping snaps, zipping a zipper, and lacing string through loops. It's also fun to add different textures like satin, wool, velvet, vinyl, and even metallic fabric.

Make a fanciful ornament with a miniature flower pot, dried flowers, a little feather bird, and a length of raffia. Use a glue gun to attach the dried flowers three-quarters of the way around the opening of the flower pot. Glue the bird to look like it is perched at the mouth of the pot. Tie the raffia just under the lip of the pot, glue it in place, and form a loop so that the ornament will hang on its side. Ornaments for year-round display can also be crafted, using a glue gun,

HAND-PAINT A WOODEN BOX AND USE IT TO PRESENT A FRIEND WITH ANYTHING
FROM BLOOMING FLOWERS TO HOMEMADE BROWNIES.

with miniature twig or silk wreaths and dried flowers, seedpods, pinecones, and nuts. Add ribbons or raffia to hang them with.

🐾 *Make paper using a paper-making kit and decorate with leaf and flower impressions. Or use craft stamps or interesting paper and a laser printer to create pretty personalized stationery. You can find appropriate-size envelopes at a stationery or print shop.*

own personal touch. After a while, you'll become an expert.

To find handmade gift ideas that fit your style and abilities, spend a few evenings leafing through crafts books and magazines. Once you've found a few projects that appeal to you, try them, adding your own details and innovations to give each your

A FRAMED, HANDMADE BIRTH ANNOUNCEMENT MAKES A WONDERFUL GIFT FOR A NEW PARENT.

The Magic of Copy Machines

Handmade gifts don't have to be old-fashioned and homey. Why not use the wonderful high-tech resources so readily available to us now? Your local print shop will show you how easy it is to make calendars, note cards, stationery, and even posters using color copies of your favorite photos and paper mementos like postcards, brochures, and newspaper or magazine clippings.

A wall calendar illustrated with color copies of photos makes a delightful gift for grandparents, godparents, and relatives as well as close friends, teachers, or colleagues. You don't have to limit yourself to one photo per page, either. Create color collages of your photos with decorative borders, embellishments, fanciful drawings, funny dialogue balloons, and descriptive captions.

With color (or even black-and-white) copiers, you can make note cards, stationery, or even wrapping paper using photos or other images that have social meaning for the recipients. Embellish with trims, rubber-stamping, hand coloring, or whatever strikes your fancy.

You can use the magic of photo-transferring to copy old photos or images onto fabric, too, from which you may a fashion a special pillow or quilt.

In chapter 6, you'll find ideas for combining technology and the written word to make people feel important and wonderful.

41

Gifts That Grow

He who plants a tree, he plants love,
Tents of coolness spreading out above
Wayfarers he may not live to see.
Gifts that grow are best.

—*Lucy Larcom*

*True isn't much
that I can do,
But I can share
my flowers with you...
And sometimes share
your burdens, too...*

❧

Maude V. Preston

hen a woman from my neighborhood died tragically at the age of forty-one, leaving four very young children, her many friends wanted to create an enduring memorial to her. On a chilly day in the fall, a group of parents and children gathered on a small hillside at her children's school to plant five hundred daffodil bulbs. The following spring the daffodils pushed their way through the cold earth, and as they opened their cheery yellow trumpets, the entire community was reminded of Mary Ellen. And every year, as the daffodils prosper and spread, her legacy will live on.

For centuries, people have used plants as symbols of their emotions and thoughts. Over time, many plants—especially flowers—have been endowed with special meanings, so that a gift of them can relay without words what is uppermost in the giver's heart or on his or her mind.

In this chapter, we'll look at ways that trees, shrubs, flowers, and bulbs can be used to express ourselves, to share love, and to make others feel good. There are also hints for how to "package" seeds, bulbs, and cuttings from favorite plants; tips on tiny forcing jars and simple vases; and various ways to use nursery catalogs, gardening books, and other horticultural items to bring the special joy of growing things into others' lives.

A gift of flowers or plants is delightfully apropos for most any occasion. Births,

43

deaths, and noteworthy accomplishments are commemorated and acknowledged with flowers. Thanks are said and good wishes shared when we offer a floral gesture. Though we most often give flowers to women and girls, there's no good reason why we shouldn't do the same for the men in our lives. Most boys, however, remain less likely to appreciate the gift of a bouquet.

Here are some ways you can express yourself with flowers or plants:

🌸 *When you receive a bouquet of flowers from a friend, save a particularly beautiful bloom to press in a heavy book. (Put it between two pieces of waxed paper to avoid staining the pages.) When the flower is fully dry, enclose it in a note to your friend.*

🌸 *Save seeds from favorite flowers in pretty, decorative envelopes to share with friends who garden. Write directions for sowing them, then take a photo of the blooms growing in your own garden or from the pages of a catalog or magazine and paste these on the envelope. Forget-me-not seeds are especially lovely to share with special friends, particularly those whom you rarely see but who are important to you. They can be scattered on loose soil and if given enough water and warmth will germinate within a week or so. Their dear, bright blue blooms will appear in the spring about the same time as tulips bloom.*

45

ANTIQUE GARDENING BOOKS TIED UP WITH RIBBON MAKE THE PERFECT GIFT FOR GARDEN LOVERS YEAR ROUND.

🌺 *Collect acorns from a venerable old oak tree in your town and put a few in a small wooden box lined with moss or raffia. This makes a lovely gift for friends who are moving away. Given the right soil and light conditions, the acorns will actually germinate and will eventually become young oaks.*

🌺 *When someone admires a certain plant in your garden, make a cutting or a division, put it in a small terra-cotta pot, and hand deliver it to his or her home.*

🌺 *When a talented florist died, her family gave out lily bulbs to all who attended her memorial service. The lily is an exquisite flower that will bloom year after year. It was a fine symbol of the beauty she had created for others during her life. Sharing bulbs is also an appropriate gesture for guests at various occasions.*

🌺 *Plant a tree to celebrate a marriage, an anniversary, or the birth of a child, or to remember someone who has died. If you can't plant the tree on your own property, find a park, arboretum, school, or playground that will appreciate the donation of a tree. Have a plaque made to distinguish the tree and organize a little ceremony for the planting. Select a long-lived species like oak, beech, pine, or redwood with the hope that the tree will outlive you, your children, and your grandchildren. Perhaps this gesture will inspire others to commemorate occasions in the same way.*

🌺 *Give bulbs to children and teach them how nature has designed the bulb to store the plant's energy in the winter so that it can come alive again in the spring.*

🌺 *Buy inexpensive forcing jars and add a crocus or hyacinth bulb to each one, tying a*

IN LIEU OF PLANTING A TREE TO COMMEMORATE A SPECIAL PERSON OR EVENT, PRESENT A LOVED ONE WITH A "MINIATURE"—IN THE FORM OF A TOPIARY.

> *The fragrance always*
> *remains in the hand*
> *that gives the rose.*
>
> *Heda Bejar*

bit of ribbon or raffia around the neck of the jar. Present these as thank-you gifts to volunteers, as a cheerful memento for someone in the hospital or recuperating at home, or as a "just thinking of you" present for a friend or loved one.

Collect pretty vases, baskets, and attractive old jars to fill with flowers from your garden and, give to visitors, or to take along with you when you visit neighbors or friends.

IN WINTER, PLANT GRASS SEED IN A PLASTIC-LINED BOX OR BASKET FILLED WITH SOIL. KEEP IT WARM AND MOIST. ONCE THE GRASS HAS SPROUTED, GIVE THE BOX TO A FRIEND WHO MISSES BEING OUTDOORS. HOUSEBOUND CATS WILL LOVE THIS, TOO!

The Language of Flowers

Plants and flowers have held special meanings since humans began cultivating them. In ancient Egypt, the palm tree symbolized fertility while the cypress stood for mortality and eternity. In classical times, the branches of olive trees represented peace. In medieval gardens, roses were thought to portray divine love. The Victorians established an elaborate "language" of flowers that corresponded with the romantic tastes of that period.

We can borrow from the past by adopting horticultural symbolism when we give plants as gifts, making the gift more thoughtful and meaningful.

FLOWER	*MEANING*
ALMOND FLOWER	*Hope*
BEECH TREE	*Prosperity*
BLUEBELL	*Constancy*
CHERRY TREE	*Good education*
DAFFODIL	*Regard*
FORGET-ME-NOT	*True love and remembrance*
HAWTHORN	*Hope*
HELIOTROPE	*Devotion and faithfulness*
HOLLY	*Enduring life*
NASTURTIUM	*Patriotism*
OAK	*Hospitality*
PERIWINKLE	*Pleasures of memory*
POPLAR	*Courage*
ROSE	*Love and beauty*
STRAWBERRY	*Esteem and love*
TULIP	*Fame*
WHITE CLOVER	*Think of me*
ZINNIA	*Thoughts of absent friends*

With these horticultural symbols in mind, you might consider using them in the following ways:

🐾 *Send a friend a bouquet of zinnias or even a collection of zinnia seeds and enclose a little note that the zinnias symbolize your fond thoughts for your friend.*

🐾 *Plant a cherry tree to celebrate a graduation. This is an especially lovely gesture for a graduating class to present to its school.*

🐾 *Take an oak seedling or a basket filled with acorns to a friend's new home.*

🐾 *Give a bouquet of tulips or a collection of tulip bulbs to someone who is auditioning for a part in a play, is performing in a concert, is about to have a book published, or has sold a story to a magazine.*

🐾 *Give heliotrope (which smells like cherry pie!) as a condolence to someone who has lost a pet.*

There are many more floral meanings. Look for the writings of Lady Mary Wortley Montague, who was the first to chronicle the language of flowers in English in the early eighteenth century, and the work of Cicely Mary Barker, who wrote and illustrated the Flower Fairies *books in the 1920s.*

51

CHAPTER
5

Food for
the Soul

*Food is the most
primitive form of comfort.*

—Sheila Graham

ood has always been an essential part of any celebration. We eat in celebration of weddings, births, holidays, and accomplishments. Our happiest moments are often accompanied by special foods. Many foods are endowed with the ability to make us feel unaccountably good—in fact, some are even described as "comfort foods."

If you enjoy cooking and creating in the kitchen, you probably already know a few ways to make gifts of food. A cookbook writer and executive editor of a cooking magazine has an expansive repertoire of special gift foods. At Christmas she fixes up extraordinary gift bags filled with her own wonderful concoctions—spiced nuts, herbed goat cheese, salsa, olives, and a variety of breads. Those who have received these delectable goodie bags fervently hope that they will remain on her gift list.

Though there are times when food has unfortunate negative connotations, it is more often associated with family, friends, and celebration. The giving and sharing of food offers innumerable opportunities to make thoughtful gifts and gestures. Here are a few ways you may use food to make others feel good:

> *Love keeps the cold out better than a cloak. It serves for food and raiment.*
>
> ❧
>
> *Henry Wadsworth Longfellow*

🌸 *Assemble a collection of an adult child's favorite recipes when he or she moves into a first apartment. Write the recipes on index cards and include a few notes about your memories associated with each recipe.*

53

Amy's Favorite Garlic Mashed Potatoes

... potatoes

Aunt (Susan's) Zucchini Bread

* 8 med
* 1/2
* 1/4 c
* 2
* 1 H
* salt
* 1 medium zucchini
* grated zest of 1 lemon
* 1/2 cup whole milk
* 2 large eggs
* 3/4 cup sugar
* 1 tsp salt
* 1/4 tsp each nutmeg and cinnamon
* 1/3 cup chopped walnuts
* 2 tbs butter, softened

1. B...

1. Preheat oven to 350°F.
2. Grate the zucchini into a medium-size mixing bowl. Add lemon zest and milk (even)

54

For example: "Pam's Shortbread—You and Daddy always made this for Christmas. We'll bake some together when you visit us."

♨ Provide an entire home-cooked meal for a friend who is ill or recovering. Sometimes preparing a main dish, a vegetable, and a salad is just too much effort for someone who is not well. Deliver the meal in plastic containers that are microwave-safe, or pack in disposable ones so that your friend won't have to worry about returning the containers.

♨ Join an organization that supplies meals for homebound folks. One such group, Aid for Friends in Philadelphia, supplies volunteers with meal-size aluminum trays and asks them to simply make one extra serving of each dish when preparing dinner. Volunteer cooks place the food in the tray's compartments, freeze it, mark the ingredients on a card, and bring the trays to a central location from which other volunteers will distribute the meals.

♨ Annotate your cookbooks with the dates you first tried recipes and on which occasions you served them. For example: "11/6/97—served at Chris & Barbara's engagement dinner." These cookbooks will someday become treasured heirlooms for future generations.

WRITE DOWN YOUR FAVORITE RECIPES ON INDEX CARDS
AND PACK THEM IN AN ANTIQUE RECIPE BOX FOR A PRESENT WITH PERSONAL WARMTH.

🌸 Keep a diary of menus served on special occasions. Include in your entry the guest list, names of wines served, and even the flowers you used. This makes it possible to duplicate the original event years later, a wonderful gesture for an anniversary or a birthday.

🌸 An especially thoughtful gesture is to ship off packages of homemade cookies or brownies to young people who are at school or camp, in the military, or away from home for the first time. Pack the goodies in a tin with plenty of waxed paper and send them by one of the overnight or second-day services to ensure they arrive fresh. Be sure to send enough for sharing!

🌸 Bake cookies for people who do nice things for you: the crossing guard or bus driver who watches out for your children, your doctor's nurse or dentist's hygienist, a particularly helpful bank employee, or your child's soccer coach.

🌸 Use cookie cutters to fashion French toast or pancakes in appropriate shapes for holidays and special occasions—hearts for Valentine's Day, shamrocks on St. Patrick's Day, and so on. Do the same with sandwiches. Children and the young at heart will appreciate your effort.

🌸 Invite the birthday girl or boy to create the birthday dinner menu. No matter how young or how grown-up, the birthday honoree would no doubt love to have his or her favorites served.

🌸 If you make your own jams, vinegars, flavored oils, preserved fruit, dried herb bouquet garni, pickles, or other pantry item, be sure to prepare enough to give as gifts. Think about making tags or labels (this is very easy with computers and laser printers or you may enjoy writing them out the old-fashioned way), and add other decorative

A BASKET OF FRESHLY BAKED BREADS MAKES A WONDERFUL "WELCOME TO THE NEIGHBORHOOD" GIFT.

index card, a simple wire whisk or a spatula, and a bag of gourmet coffee or a selection of teas, and place it all in a basket or a vintage mixing bowl lined with a colorful dish towel.

❀ Organize a potluck dinner with a group of friends.

❀ Even if you don't cook, you can still give a gift of food: create a basket filled with savory or sweet treats from a gourmet food shop; take a friend for tea at a local tearoom; give a gift certificate for dinner or brunch at an elegant restaurant to a young couple just starting out.

packaging like raffia bows, dried flowers, bells, or tin ornaments to make the gifts even more festive.

❀ Make gift baskets with meal themes. For example, mix all the dry ingredients for your favorite pancake or waffle recipe, and heap the mix into a muslin bag closed with a rubber band and tied with decorative twine or raffia. Add a jar of blueberry preserves, honey, or the maple syrup you picked up on your vacation in Vermont. Include the pancake recipe written on an

HOMEMADE PRESERVES FROM YOUR KITCHEN TOPPED WITH DELIGHTFUL
COUNTRY FABRICS MAKE PERFECT HOUSEWARMING GIFTS.

The Gift of Words

*The human contribution is the
essential ingredient. It is only in the
giving of oneself to others
that we truly live.*

—Ethel Percy Andrus

How often do we find ourselves called upon to write a few words to praise an employee, to inspire a child, to honor a distinguished community member, to say "thank you" to a friend, or to memorialize a loved one? Even though this is a task we all must do at one time or another, for many the thought of writing or speaking a few bon mots brings on dread or even terror. Few of us are blessed with a gift for words, but we all have it within ourselves to speak or write what is in our hearts.

The key to using words in the context of a gift or thoughtful gesture is to speak or write naturally, as one would in a conversation. And to make one's words effective, it's important to resist the inhibitions that often prevent us from saying what we truly feel.

It can be helpful to begin at a library, where you'll find books of quotations. Many are indexed or organized by topic as well as author so you can search for appropriate subjects like love, motherhood, service to others, family, joy, or success. A few titles are devoted to one subject, like Maria Polushkin Robbins' *A Gardener's Bouquet of Quotations.* Search for quotes that appeal to you and that reflect the message you wish

ANTIQUE LEATHERBOUND EDITIONS OF FAVORITE BOOKS GIVE A PERSONAL LIBRARY A SPECIAL TOUCH.

> *Kindness is the sunshine in which virtue grows.*
>
> ❧
>
> *Robert G. Ingersoll*

to convey. The Bible and books of proverbs are also helpful places to start. You may find everything you want to express in one sentence from one book.

Here are a few suggestions for using words in thoughtful ways:

❧ *Instead of phoning your thanks for a gift or favor, take the extra minute or two needed to pen a short note. Always keep a supply of attractive note cards and stamps on hand, and make sure your address book is up to date.*

❧ *Include little notes with funny drawings with the lunch you pack for your child for school.*

❧ *Tuck a love letter into your spouse's briefcase or jacket pocket for a loving surprise when he or she arrives at the office.*

❧ *When you send snapshots to family or friends, write amusing captions on the back and include the date.*

❧ *Always inscribe books you give as gifts. You don't need to be clever. A simple "For Anne, with great affection" is enough. Be sure to include the date.*

❧ *When you are the host of celebratory dinners, including wedding rehearsals and receptions, retirements, anniversaries, and recognitions, you will be expected to say a few words. Your remarks need not be long but must be heartfelt. You may find something appropriate in a book of toasts (available at the library), or you might find a quote or story you can rework to fit the occasion.*

PRESENT A CHILD WHO IS GOING AWAY TO SCHOOL OR A FRIEND WHO IS MOVING AWAY WITH A SET OF ELEGANT STATIONERY TO MAKE WRITING THAT MUCH EASIER.

Riches and power are but gifts of blind fate,
whereas goodness is the result of one's own merits.
—Heloise

Computer Magic

With the proliferation of home computers, it is now easy for all of us to create special gifts with words. With the enormous selection of fonts, formats, and decorative laser printer papers it is possible for even the most inexperienced among us to design announcements, certificates, "proclamations," and official-looking documents. If you are particularly computer-phobic, you might hire your local print shop to do the job for you at a reasonable cost.

With a bit of creativity, you can invent appropriate and fun awards for volunteers, teachers, children, and friends. Your children could design an official-looking document, emblazoned with a gold seal sticker, that proclaims Sharon to be their favorite babysitter. If you are the head of a committee, you can make certificates for each member of the committee commending individual efforts. Grandma might enjoy a certificate of appreciation, and a favorite teacher would surely love a "teacher of the year" award made by a student. The possibilities are endless, as are the opportunites to make people feel special.

USE CALLIGRAPHY OR A LASER PRINTER WITH DECORATIVE FONTS
TO WRITE AN INSPIRATIONAL MESSAGE, THEN MAT AND FRAME.

65

CHAPTER
7

Special
Gestures

Sow good services;
sweet remembrances
will grow from them.

—Madame de Staël

*J*ust about every day we are presented with opportunities to make a small, thoughtful gesture that can brighten a day, lighten a burden, or simply make someone feel good. And there are always reasons to find special ways to express our care, appreciation, or concern for others. A friendly smile, a wave, or a heartfelt "thank you" are the everyday gifts we bestow on one another. And there are many ways to demonstrate what we feel in our hearts.

Perhaps a volunteer on your committee at the library has done a particularly good job and you want to let her know how much you appreciate her efforts. Or maybe your child's teacher has given him the extra bit of attention he needed during an especially difficult time. Or it could be that your elderly neighbor is desperately

If someone listens, or stretches out a hand, or whispers a kind word of encouragement, or attempts to understand a lonely person, extraordinary things begin to happen.

Loretta Girzartes

67

lonely since the death of her husband. This chapter will provide examples of ways people have shared themselves with others in simple, thoughtful ways.

Share your list of babysitters with someone new to your neighborhood. First make sure it's all right with the babysitters. Then type up the list or print it on a card so that the neighbor

*Happiness is not a goal;
it is a by-product.*

❦

Eleanor Roosevelt

can keep it on his or her bulletin board or near the phone.

🐾 Make a donation to the local animal shelter in memory of a friend's beloved pet that has just died.

🐾 If you have a friend with a terminally ill pet, offer to accompany them to the vet. Your presence will make the loss easier to bear.

🐾 Send flowers to your parents on your birthday.

🐾 When a friend is planning a wedding to which you will not be invited, offer to housesit on the big day. An empty house full of wedding gifts could be a target for thieves, so the family may feel a bit more relaxed if someone is in attendance.

🐾 Next time you run errands, check with an elderly or ill neighbor, or one with tiny children, to see if he or she needs anything mailed or picked up at the dry cleaner or from the grocery store. It will only add a few minutes to your stops but will be enormously helpful for your neighbor.

🐾 When you take public transportation, be aware of elderly, frail, or pregnant people, so you can offer your seat.

🐾 Offer to take an older neighbor, who no longer drives, with you to the shopping mall or grocery store.

🐾 Give your children prepaid telephone cards when they go away to school or camp or to visit friends. They'll feel

SPONSOR AN ANIMAL AT THE ZOO FOR AN ANIMAL-LOVING FRIEND.

WILDLIFE
CONSERVATION
SOCIETY

Sponsor-A-Species Program

Certificate of Sponsorship

presented to

Julia Patricia Bair

for generous support of

Siberian Tiger

Your contribution supports species threatened with extinction and celebrates 100 years
of conservation efforts of the Wildlife Conservation Society.

Howard

Date: May 13, 1998

more secure and are more likely to stay in touch.

🦋 When grocery stores offer a percentage of the cash register tapes for not-for-profit groups, save the tapes and donate them to community groups.

🦋 Clip coupons for items your family and friends use and send them along.

🦋 Give a respite to a friend who is the caretaker of an elderly or ill person who cannot be left alone. Offer to relieve him or her for an hour or two so he or she can have a little break. Do the same for a sleep-deprived new mother so that she might have a nap.

🦋 Make a point of stopping at a lemonade stand run by small children. The five minutes and fifty cents you spend will be worth a fortune in good memories to them.

AT THE END OF THE SCHOOL YEAR, WRITE A LETTER TO A BELOVED TEACHER
EXPRESSING PRAISE AND GRATITUDE FOR A JOB WELL DONE.

WILDLIFE
CONSERVATION
SOCIETY

Sponsor-A-Species Program

Certificate of Sponsorship

presented to

Julia Patricia Bain

for generous support of

Siberian Tiger

contribution supports species threatened with extinction and celebrates 100 years of conservation efforts of the Wildlife Conservation Society.

May 13, 1998

Howard _____

Bronx, New York, Jr., Chairman

Wildlife Conservation Society

more secure and are more likely to stay in touch.

When grocery stores offer a percentage of the cash register tapes for not-for-profit groups, save the tapes and donate them to community groups.

Clip coupons for items your family and friends use and send them along.

Give a respite to a friend who is the care-taker of an elderly or ill person who cannot be

left alone. Offer to relieve him or her for an hour or two so he or she can have a little break. Do the same for a sleep-deprived new mother so that she might have a nap.

Make a point of stopping at a lemon-ade stand run by small children. The five minutes and fifty cents you spend will be worth a fortune in good mem-ories to them.

AT THE END OF THE SCHOOL YEAR, WRITE A LETTER TO A BELOVED TEACHER
EXPRESSING PRAISE AND GRATITUDE FOR A JOB WELL DONE.

70

- *Start a conversation with the person ahead of or behind you in line at the grocery store. For some lonely people, those few minutes of friendly chatter may be all the human contact they have in a day.*

- *When you have received particularly good service from an employee of a store, a business, or an agency, write a letter of praise to the owner or manager. Too often the only letters supervisors receive are complaints. People deserve to hear the good news, too.*

- *Offer to teach a friend's teenager to drive. Often there is too much tension between parent and child for driving lessons to be without conflict.*

- *Lend out books that you've enjoyed to friends and neighbors. (Be sure to put your name in them so that your books will be returned.)*

- *Offer to take your elderly or ill neighbor's pet for a walk, to the vet, or to the groomer.*

- *Clean a close friend's refrigerator or oven while he or she is away.*

- *Give a potted plant to welcome a new colleague to your workplace and brighten his or her desk.*

- *Organize a night on the town with a lively group and invite a lonely single or divorced friend.*

*The richest gifts
we can bestow
are the least marketable.*

Henry David Thoreau